Creative Jams and Preserves

EASY RECIPES HANDCRAFTED BY YOU

RENEE POTTLE

HESTIA'S HEARTH * KENNEWICK, WASHINGTON

Creative Jams and Preserves
EASY RECIPES HANDCRAFTED BY YOU

Hestia's Hearth LLC
PO Box 7059
Kennewick, WA 99336
Email: info@SeedtoPantry.com
www.SeedtoPantry.com
ISBN: 978-0-9760137-5-4

Introduction

Some things shouldn't be rushed; falling in love, artisan bread, and homemade sweet spreads among them.

Yes, we can quickly cook up a pot of berries, stir in some commercially prepared pectin, and have a few jars of jam or jelly in minutes. But there's something to be said for taking our time and coaxing those same berries into a thickened concoction of their own.

Are you new to no-pectin spreads? If so, you are in for a treat. Cooking fruit and sugar for a longer time intensifies the flavor, giving jams and preserves a concentrated burst of apricot or blueberry or cherry that can't be found in quick-cooking pectin-added jams.

These are the recipes your grandmother, and her grandmother, prepared. Stirring a pot of peaches or berries until they thicken connects you to those who have come before you.

Creative, no-pectin spreads turn today's world of *fast food, but not necessarily good food* on its head. Celebrate real food with long-cooking jams, preserves, fruit butters, and other sweet spreads!

Table of Contents

CHAPTER FIVE – PRESERVES RECIPES   89

CHAPTER SIX – SYRUP, JELLY, AND CONSERVES RECIPES   103

CHAPTER SEVEN – RESOURCES   122

CHAPTER ONE

Canning Basics

It is easy to can your own jams, jellies and other sweet spreads. You don't have to be an expert. You don't need 25 years of cooking experience. You don't have to slave over a hot stove for hours or make 100 jars of jam.

There are a few basics to learn first, but so few you can start canning today! You do need a stove of some sort. You do need to be able to stir the pot (literally not figuratively). You do need a few supplies and some basic safety reminders. You will find it all explained here.

So, grab some berries and a jar or two and start making jam! I guarantee it will be the start of a beautiful love affair with canning.

Needed Canning Equipment

Does this describe you? You are ready to start exploring how to can food at home, but are scared off by all the new equipment that seems necessary? The good news - water bath canning really doesn't require spending lots of money. In fact, you probably already have almost everything you need right at home, and can purchase the remainder for under $50. Here's how:

Necessary Equipment

In my opinion, there are only three items you *have* to purchase for water bath canning, assuming you already have access to a stove, a ladle, and a long-handled spoon:

- **Canning Jars** – approved canning jars with two- piece lids. Your Mom may have used empty mayonnaise or pickle jars. Please don't! Commercial canning is a different process, and those jars are not designed for the home canning process. At best, you'll end up with lots of broken jars. Or worse; broken jars and injuries from glass shards.

- **Jar Lifter** – I love this handy implement. There is just no other way to effectively remove hot jars from a water bath canner.

- **Canning Rack** – Although a purchased canner is not absolutely necessary (see below), you will need some sort of rack to keep the jars off the bottom of the pot. Most canners come with an aluminum rack. This works great, but will rust over time. If you are planning to do a lot of water bath canning, treat yourself and splurge on a stainless-steel rack. It took me years to do this. Don't be a cheapskate like me!

Helpful Equipment

Although not absolutely necessary, you really should have this equipment for effective canning:

- **Water Bath Canner** – Really, you can use any large stock pot for canning, as long as it is deep enough to cover the jars with 2 inches of water. But most stock pots are tall and narrow or short and wide, neither of which meets our needs when canning. Water Bath Canners are tall enough to cover the jars and wide enough to allow us to process up to 7 jars at a time. Plus, they are really inexpensive, only about $25.

- **Canning Funnel** – You can fill jars without a funnel, but using one makes the job easier and less messy.

- **Paper Towels** – Probably already in your kitchen, a moist paper towel is the easiest way to wipe jar lips before the two-piece lids. You could use cheesecloth or another clean, lint free cotton cloth, but paper towels make the job easier.

Desired Equipment

Some equipment is not necessary, but will make the whole canning process more enjoyable:

- **Bubble Remover** – This implement is specifically designed to remove bubbles from filled jars. Most often used when canning fruits or pickles. Any long, non-metallic device can be used, but the bubble remover is thin and thus more effective.

- **Dishwasher** – Do you remember Grandma sterilizing her canning jars in a big pot of boiling water on the stove? You can still do it that way, but I prefer to run the jars through the dishwasher. As long as the canning jars and lids are clean, and the processing time for your project is at least 10 minutes, it's no longer necessary to sterilize canning jars before use.

- **Towel** –I place old dishtowels on the counter to cushion the jars. The towels keep the jars from slipping while they are being filled, and then insulates the hot jars after processing.

- **Camp Stove** – A camp stove may fall into the **Necessary Equipment** category if you have a glass-top stove. But even if that isn't a concern, a camp stove can make canning on a hot summer day a much more enjoyable experience. Using a camp stove moves the processing heat out of your kitchen and gives you an excuse to spend the time outdoors enjoying the day.

Reaching the Right Consistency

Making jam or jelly with prepared pectin is supposed to be an easy project. Add the pectin, bring to a boil, boil for 2 minutes and voila! Perfectly prepared jam. It doesn't always work like this, but basically you, the cook, don't have to think too much about it.

Using the natural pectin found in your ingredients though requires a bit more finesse. Don't worry, it still isn't a difficult process and the little bit of extra work is worth the added flavor.

There are a few ways to test jams and jellies for correct consistency. Use whichever one of these methods work best for you.

- **The plate method.** I used this method for decades with excellent results. Drop some of the cooking jam onto a glass plate and put it in the refrigerator for a minute. If the jam sets up to the level you like (there is no such thing as the "right" level, only the level you prefer) remove the cooking jam from the heat and ladle it into jars.

- **Cold plate method.** Similar to above, cool a glass plate in the freezer until it is cold. Drop some of the cooking jam onto the plate. Draw a spoon through the jam. If the line stays separated, the jam is done.

- **Spoon method.** Using a metal spoon, stir the cooking jam and then lift it out of the mixture. If the jam comes off the spoon in a sheet, it has successfully thickened. It may be difficult for you to correctly judge the thickness if you are new to jam making. I also find berry jams difficult to judge this way and end up over cooking them.

- **Temperature method.** This method is the easiest, with a caveat. Jam is usually set when the temperature reaches 8-9 degrees above the temperature of boiling water. Water usually boils at 212 degrees, but not always. Several things can affect the temperature, including altitude and barometric pressure. So, if you choose to use this method, check today's boiling water temperature first. Otherwise you may end up with burnt jam from cooking too long.

Jar Sizes

Canning jars come in all different shapes and sizes. Which size works best for your project? The most common jars here in the United States are Ball® and Kerr® brand jars.

- **Quarter-pint:** Tiny four-ounce jars are perfect for gifting jams and other sweet spreads. They are also a good size for single households where a larger jar of jam might sit in the refrigerator for a long time. I especially like to make my Blueberry Cointreau Preserves and Spirited Apricot Cherry Butter in these cute little jars. Process for the same length of time as half-pint jars.

- **Half-Pint:** Most people use these eight-ounce jars for sweet spreads. Eight-ounce jars come in several different varieties; Quilted jars with beveled-like sides, regular clear, straight-sided jars and specialty jars that are rounded or have squared sides.

- **Three-Quarter Pint:** Twelve-ounce jars can be difficult to find, but they are the perfect size for pickled asparagus or pickled beans. I like to use these jars for my Apricot Syrup.

- **Pint:** A full 16 ounces, pint jars come in regular mouth and large mouth shapes. Some people like to make jelly in pint jars. For most of us though, pint jars are too large for sweet spreads. Regular mouth pints are good for salsa or tomato sauce. Wide mouth pint jars work nicely for pickles.

- **Quart:** Quart jars are just too large for sweet spreads to be processed at home. But quart jars are the perfect size for canned tomatoes or fruits, or for pickle spears.

Several European style jars available online. I am particularly fond of Weck tulip jars and Bormioli Rocco Quattro Stagioni jars, but save them for gift-giving as they are more expensive than Ball® and Kerr® brand jars. Both, along with many other brands, can be ordered at Amazon.com.

Water Bath Canning Basics

Water Bath Canning is appropriate for high acid foods only.

> *High acid + boiling water + processing time = destruction of harmful bacteria and molds.*

Most berries and fruits, most pickles, jams, jellies and other soft spreads are considered high acid foods.

Step by Step Instructions:

1. Heat water to boiling in a tea kettle or saucepan.

2. Fill canner half-full of warm water, or enough water to cover jars by at least one inch of water. Heat to 140 – 180 degrees.

3. Add ¼ cup of white vinegar to canner. The vinegar keeps jars bright and shiny and also slows canner rack rusting.

4. Use clean canning jars, lids, and rings that have been washed in the dishwasher if your recipe processing time is at least 10 minutes. Alternatively, use jars sterilized for 10 minutes in boiling water. Jars MUST be sterilized if your recipe processing time is less than 10 minutes, (e.g. jelly). If using sterilized jars, lids and rings must also be sterilized in boiling water.

5. Fill jars leaving recommended amount of head space. Most jams require ¼ inch head space, most pickles require ½ inch head space.

6. Wipe jar lips with a clean damp cloth or paper towel.

7. Place lids on filled jars.

8. Hand tighten rings on jars. Don't over-tighten!

9. Load filled jars into the canner rack. Conversely, if your canner rack is already in the canner, load jars into the rack using a jar lifter.

10. Place canner rack and jars in canner. Make sure water is 1 – 2 inches over top of jars. If not, add boiling water started in Step 1.

11. Bring water to a boil. Cover, turn down heat slightly (it must remain boiling) and process for length of time your recipe recommends.

12. When processing time is complete; turn off burner, carefully remove cover, and remove jars using a jar lifter. DO NOT tip jars to displace water on lids. The water will evaporate.

13. Place hot jars on a towel to cool. Let sit for 12 to 24 hours.

14. When cool, remove rings, wipe and label jars and store in a cool, dark place. Jars that did not seal must be stored in the refrigerator.

Using Canners on a Glass Top Stove

Earlier this year my old stove up and died. It was time to replace it, but of course I wanted something the stove manufacturers don't make; an electric slide-in convection stove with top coils so I can safely use my water bath canner. After many hours of research (sometimes I over-analyze a wee bit) I found:

- a slide-in convection stove
- a slide-in with coil top
- a convection with coil top

Sadly, I could not find a single appliance that included all of the above. Until a random remark. "Oh," the salesperson said, "all of the new glass-top stoves are safe for canning." I was delighted, but skeptical.

So, it was back to Google (how did we live before Google?). I looked up several different stoves online. And according to the owner's manuals, they are all safe for home canning. With a couple of caveats:

> *1. The canner must have a flat bottom. That means my old enamel canner with bottom ridges will have to be replaced.*
>
> *2. The canner should not overhang the burner by more than ½ inch on any side. Therefore, they don't recommend large water bath canners. This will make it difficult to process large batches of quart sized jars unless I continue to do those outside on a camp burner.*

Finding the Correct Canner

This step was much more difficult than I expected. Not only did I need a flat bottom canner, it could not be larger than 11 inches in diameter since my largest burner is 10 inches.

I finally decided to purchase a **16-quart stainless steel stock pot**. It has a flat bottom, is only 11 inches in diameter, and won't rust! Plus, it is small enough to be manageable but large enough to process a two layers of jam jars at once. As a stock pot, it also will easily do double duty. It is the perfect size for making soup this winter when the whole family comes over.

Finding the Correct Canning Rack

Next, I tackled a canning rack. This was even more difficult than finding a water bath canner. But I am very pleased with a reversible canning rack from Sur la Table. It is heavier and of higher quality than most traditional basket type canner racks.

Other Canning Options

Using the stock pot/canning rack combination means that my stove top will not be harmed from too much trapped heat and that the canning process will safely stay at a boiling temperature.

Jarden Home Brands (Ball®) has recently come out with an electric water bath canner. It is reasonably priced but has mixed reviews. It might be the perfect option for those of you who have older glass top stoves, or who don't want to do a lot of canning on a glass top stove.

As I mention in *The Confident Canner*, most Frigidaire® brand stoves have long been approved for water bath canning. However, the "no more than 1-inch diameter" rule has always applied, so beware that your canner may not work with your stove top.

Of course, a three-legged camp stove is still a good option for water bath canning. And it allows us to enjoy the great summer weather while canning!

You could also use the burner on your gas grill. It's like having your own old-time summer kitchen. Or use a separate electric burner. Some people have good luck using a one or two burner portable electric range. Read the directions first to make sure they are approved for large pots.

A Word of Caution

Don't forget that you should always check your stove manufacturer's operating guide before deciding to can on a glass top stove. Cook tops that are not approved for canning may crack or even shatter. Heat trapped under the canner will cause the cook top to break. If the stove manufacturer recommends NOT using the stove for canning, your warranty will be voided.

Even if the top doesn't break (and who wants to chance it!), a canner full of water may never come to a boil, or it won't be able to hold a boil. This is because most canners have bottom ridges, thus not enough of the canner comes in contact with heat. No lasting boil means that the canned food items are not processed correctly.

Open Kettle Canning

Many of us have fond memories of canning and preserving beside our mothers and grandmothers.

We pass down family canning recipes (Russian Bear pickles and chokecherry jelly in my family) and preferences. Canning and preserving stories are the fabric that binds multiple generations together. I love the idea that my grandchildren may someday make the same recipes with their grandchildren that I made with my grandmother.

But times change. Most family jam or pickle recipes can be updated to meet our safer, more modern techniques, just don't forget that the process used needs to be updated too.

What is open kettle canning?

One old-time process that is still hanging around is open kettle canning. What is open kettle canning? If you ever watched your mom pour hot jam into jars, cover and invert them, that is open kettle canning. It is basically the process of letting the hot food help form a jar seal, but leaving out the water bath or pressure canning safety step.

Is open kettle canning safe?

Needless to say, open kettle canning is not safe. Jams and jellies made using this non-process have a high spoilage rate, ruining your hard work! What's even more distressing is that a non-processed, vacuum sealed jar is the perfect environment for botulism spores to multiply. Remember, just because a jar is sealed doesn't mean that it is safe.

So, it is time for this old technique to die now. Remember all canned products must be processed, either by water bath or pressure canning – according to the recipe directions. If your old family recipe calls for the open kettle technique, find a similar approved recipe in a modern canning guide and follow that. And write down the updated process – your grandchildren will thank you some day!

Using Steam Canners

For years we have been told not to use steam canners. Even though they can be found on store shelves and in gardening catalogs, they had never actually been deemed a safe way to process home canned goods. Which is why I drilled holes in my steam canner and turned it into a planter.

But now a new study shows that steam canners *are* safe – when used following these guidelines.

- Only use with high acid foods, i.e. the same foods you would process in a water bath canner.

- Only use with recipes that have been approved for use with a water bath canner. Recipes that come with the steam canner instruction booklet may not be safe.

- Heat jars before filling, and don't let the filled jars cool for very long before processing.

- Don't use jars larger than 1 quart in size.

- Start the processing time once you have a steady stream of true steam (212 degrees).

- Don't forget to adjust for altitude. The usual adjustment is to increase processing times by 5 minutes for each 1000 additional feet in elevation. However, it is always best to check safe processing times for elevations over 1000 feet with your local extension office.

- Only use canning recipes that call for a processing time of 45 minutes or less.

- As with other canned goods, processed jars should be cooled on a counter top in still air, not in the refrigerator.

As noted by Sean Timberlake, food preservation expert at **Punk Domestics**, using a steam canner may be very helpful in areas that are affected by extreme drought and water restrictions. Steam canners use much less water than water bath canners.

Personally, I find that to be the only benefit of using a steam canner. I use clean canning jars directly from the dishwasher, but they aren't always still warm. And I have no interest in heating up another pot to keep the jars hot.

Since I live in a very dry area, steaming anything is often a lesson in frustration as I constantly have to add water to keep it from boiling dry. That means each time water is added to a steam canner the processing time would start over.

So, while using a steam canner might be perfect for you, I guess mine will remain a planter.

How to Label Your Home Canned Creations

A few years ago, my mother-in-law bought us a jar of homemade onion relish at the local harvest fair. The relish certainly looked festive, but we didn't dare eat it. Why? Because we knew nothing about it except that it was homemade and in a mason jar.

The label said, *onion relish*. Nothing else. What was it made from? Had it been processed? How old was it? Who made it? It included no information. It may have been perfectly safe. It may have been the best onion relish on the planet. Sadly, we will never know because it went in the trash, unopened.

Don't let the same thing happen to your home canned gifts. Your homemade gifts come from the heart, and we both know they are better than any commercially made item. So, once you gather the harvest, find the perfect recipe, make your special raspberry jam or green tomato salsa, process the jars and lovingly decorate them, don't forget to add a label.

What Should the Label Include?

- **Product Name:** You recognize your savory Asian Apricot Sauce by sight, but Grandpa Joe might not. If he thinks it is jam and spreads it on his morning English muffin, you may lose a fan!

- **Date:** Home canned goods are best used within a year. Add the date to show it is freshly made.

- **Recipe Source:** Remember, a safe recipe is a tested recipe! Even long-time family favorites need to be based on safe, tested recipes. Identifying your recipe source shows that the gift is a safe food product.

- **Ingredients:** People are allergic to all kinds of things. Avoid making your gift recipients ill – list the ingredients.

- **Processing Method and Time:** Water bathed? Pressure canned? Include the method used on your label, and the processing time. Was your jam water bathed for 10 minutes? Include it.

- **Name:** Don't forget to add your name!

Do I Always Have to Label My Canned Goods?

No. If you are using the items yourself, in your own home, and have kept track of the above information in your trusty **Canning Journal** (you are keeping a journal, right?!), you do not have to add a label.

But.... If you give items as gifts, a label is necessary.

I Can't Fit All That Information on a Tiny Label!

Neither can I. That's why I usually write the item name on the top of the jar, and include all the information on a separate tag. There are lots of creative ways to do this:

- Type the information, print it out on card stock, punch a hole in one end and tie it to the jar.

- Type the information, print it out on an adhesive mailing label, and attach it to a purchased gift tag.

- Practice your beautiful handwriting onto specialty paper and glue it down the length of the jar.

- Include a beautiful card listing the labeling information with the canned goods in a basket.

Home canned goods are wonderful gifts. Label yours to ensure that they are enjoyed as they should be!

Date: September 22, 2013   - Blue Ribbon Corn Relish
Recipe Source:
        Better Homes and Gardens Canning Publication, 2011
Ingredients: Fresh corn kernals, celery, bell peppers,
            onions, cider vinegar, sugar, dry mustard, salt,
                celery seeds. turmeric, cornstarch

Water Bath: 15 minutes

Pressure Canned:
                    by Renee Pottle
                www.SeedToPantry.com

CHAPTER TWO
Troubleshooting

    Occasionally it happens to us all - a batch of over-cooked or under-cooked jam. Don't worry; usually the problem can be fixed with just a few steps.

How to Repair Overcooked Jam

One question I am asked over and over – "how do I fix my overcooked jam?"

It's frustrating. You spend time, money, and energy to lovingly make a batch of beautiful jam. You have visions of tucking it into Christmas baskets or spooning it atop homemade biscuits. Your family is impressed by the sheer variety of jammy combinations; apricot-raspberry, apple-pear, cherry-lime, combinations you won't find on any grocery shelves. And then you open a jar and find that it is thick. Not just thick, but gloopy – impossible to spread with a knife, almost gummy candy. Ahhhhhh!

You are in good company. Most of us overcook a batch or two of sweet spreads every year. I personally have no problems making peach jam, apricot jam or plum anything, but have great difficulties with berry or cherry jams. I know people who are the exact opposite and struggle with stone fruit spreads. There are some ways to salvage overcooked jam. You usually don't have to toss the whole thing, unless….

It is scorched. If the jam tastes burnt, you might as well face facts and just get it out of your sight and into the garbage. There is no way to rehabilitate scorched jam. If it isn't scorched though, here are some ideas to try:

- Slowly heat it in the microwave, a few seconds at a time, and then use as usual.

- If it is still too thick, add some water while heating it in the microwave and then use it as a delicious and unusual pancake or ice cream syrup. (Really, where else would you find Orange Marmalade Ice Cream Sundaes? Your family will think that you are brilliant. And you are!)

- Whisk some overcooked jam together with vinegar and tomato sauce to make your own BBQ sauce.

- Spoon it into the center of homemade jam surprise muffins. I often use up my overcooked jam tucked into the center of peanut butter muffins.

- Make your own version of Chicken Cherries Jubilee. (See Resources section).

- Melt the jam in the microwave and brush it over a freshly baked pound cake or bar cookies. It adds flavor and helps keep the baked goods moist.

- Add a spoonful to stir-fried vegetables for a flavor boost.

- Beat some into buttercream frosting and spread on cupcakes.

Can you feel your frustrations melting away? Good. You may decide that overcooked jam is your cooking secret ingredient, and next year you'll be intentionally overcooking it. At least, that is what you can tell people!

How to Repair Under-Cooked Jam

There are a variety of reasons why your jams and preserves might not set. With long-cooking jams fruit acidity is very important. Some fruits are just not acid enough to ever set unless pectin is added (melons for example).

But sometimes the fruit is just too ripe so the acid level is a little low. Sometimes the jam wasn't cooked long enough to set. Cooking time fluctuates with the weather, so even if your raspberry jam last week cooked in 30 minutes, this week it may take 40 minutes or even 20 minutes. So, here's what to do:

- Spoon all the undercooked jam into a large sauce pot.
- Add 1 tsp lemon juice for each cup of jam.
- Bring to a boil and cook until jam sets.
- Remove from heat and pour into clean jars.
- Seal and process in a water bath canner for 10 – 15 minutes.

CHAPTER THREE
Jam Recipes

If we are *in a jam* we're in a real muddle. Jam in a jar is no different. Technically *jam* is a mixture of crushed or finely chopped fruit, muddled together in a gel but still spreadable.

Make your own jam muddle by following these tips:

- Rub butter or margarine around the top inside edge of the saucepan. The fat keeps the jam from boiling over. Boiling jam all over the stove is a mess. Sadly, I know this because I have had to clean up sticky, burnt jam more than once.

- Wash half-pint canning jars and 2-piece lids in the dishwasher. It's a good idea to wash 1 or 2 more jars than you think you need. Hold the clean jars in the dishwasher until ready to use.

- Watch out for spitting. The closer the jam gets to the gelling point, the further it will spit – and it's hot!

- Cook all of your sweet spreads in small batches. Don't be tempted to double the recipe. Doubling a sweet spread recipe often leads to a sticky, overcooked lumpy mess or a syrupy undercooked jam.

Mango Jam with Star Anise

Do you ever miss canning during the winter months? I sure do. But once spring starts to show its head, I find myself canning jam – a lot.

Mangoes are available all year at the grocery store, but they are usually hard and tasteless in the winter. They look good, but go from not-ripe-at-all to brown and bruised, never reaching the juicy sweetness that makes mango one of my favorite fruits.

Once the weather starts to warm a bit, the mangoes improve in quality. There are thousands of mango varieties, although only two or three are ever available at my local grocery stores. It doesn't matter, they are all good and will all work in this recipe. Use some very ripe mangoes and at least one that is soft, but still a bit under-ripe. This combination assures that there is enough acid for the jam to set.

What is Star Anise?

Have you ever seen a star-shaped spice berry? That is star anise. It comes from an evergreen plant and has a resinous quality similar to other evergreen berries; e.g. capers, pine nuts, juniper berries.

Star anise has a subtle, herb-licorice flavor. Like anise seed it is used in both savory and sweet foods. But the two are not related and really cannot be substituted for each other. Star anise is like anise's doppelgänger, there are some similarities but they aren't interchangeable.

INGREDIENTS

- 1 CUP WATER
- 2 STAR ANISE
- 4 CUPS CHOPPED MANGO, ABOUT 3 LARGE MANGOES
- 2 CUPS GRANULATED SUGAR

1. Add star anise and water to a small saucepan to make an infusion. Bring to a boil. Remove from heat and let sit for at least 20 minutes. Remove star anise.

2. In a large Dutch oven, combine mango and infused water.

3. Simmer until mango is tender, adding small amounts of water to prevent sticking if necessary.

4. Lightly mash cooked mango with a potato masher.

5. Add sugar. Stir over medium heat until sugar has melted.

6. Turn up heat to medium-high. Cook rapidly until mixture gels (mounds on a spoon). This may happen before 220 degrees as mango has lots of pectin.

7. Spoon hot jam into prepared jars, leaving ¼ inch head space.

8. Wipe the lip of each jar with a damp paper towel, top the jars with a lid and a lid ring.

9. Process the jars in a water bath canner for 10 minutes. Remove and let cool completely.

Makes about 3 half-pints.

Apricot Jam

Have you ever had a ripe apricot, fresh from the tree? Do you remember the sensation of biting into its velvety flesh? The sweet-tart flavor on your tongue? The juice dribbling down your chin? If not, this should become one of your goals in life!

Apricots do not ripen once picked off the tree, and ripe apricots don't travel well since they are delicate and easily bruised. So, if you live far from an apricot growing area, the fruit that adorns the grocery produce section is a poor relation of the real thing.

Maybe you, like me, are lucky enough to live near an apricot orchard. Some years the apricots are fleeting, going from the first ripe blush of sweetness to too soft and over-ripe in a matter of days. Other years the weather cooperates and the fruit ripens over a few weeks. Either way, the season is never long enough but I almost always snag at least one 20-pound box to make apricot jam. There isn't another fruit with apricot's fresh flavor. Pineapple, mango, and peaches are all similar, but lack the tartness that makes apricots unique.

If you aren't able to purchase ripe apricots, maybe it's time to plant your own tree. The season is a short one, but there are apricot varieties that will grow in even cold areas and as far north as the USDA Zone 5.

INGREDIENTS

- 8 CUPS CHOPPED, SLIGHTLY CRUSHED APRICOTS
- ¼ CUP LEMON JUICE
- 6 CUPS GRANULATED SUGAR

1. Add the apricots, sugar, and lemon juice to a large Dutch oven.

2. Slowly bring the mixture to a boil over medium heat stirring until the sugar is dissolved.

3. Turn the heat up a little and cook rapidly, stirring often to prevent sticking, until the jam reaches the gelling point, about 25 minutes.

4. Spoon hot jam into prepared jars, leaving ¼ inch head space.

5. Wipe the lip of each jar with a damp paper towel, top the jars with a lid and a lid ring.

6. Process the jars in a water bath canner for 15 minutes. Remove and let cool completely.

Makes about 9 half-pints.

Raspberry-Apricot Jam

Last summer I snagged a 27-pound box of large, juicy, luscious apricots from the local fruit orchard. The apricots suffered from sun scald, which affected their beauty but not their taste. They were too large, too ripe, and had too many scars to can as halves, so I got busy turning them into something else.

I made apricot jam. And more apricot jam. Apricot Amaretto jam. Spirited Apricot-Cherry Butter. Two kinds of Apricot Sorbet. I froze some apricot puree to make apricot syrup later. And the grandchildren and I ate lots of fresh apricots.

As in previous years, I also made this delicious raspberry-apricot jam. The combination is a family favorite. Tart apricots temper raspberry's richness, enhancing both flavors.

Fun Fact: According to Greek Mythology, raspberries became red when the nymph Ida pricked her finger while picking berries for Jupiter. The white berries then turned red.

INGREDIENTS

- 7 CUPS RASPBERRIES
- 2 CUPS CHOPPED APRICOTS
- 6 CUPS GRANULATED SUGAR

1. Add the apricots, raspberries, and sugar to a large Dutch oven.

2. Slowly bring the mixture to a boil over medium heat stirring until the sugar is dissolved.

3. Turn the heat up a little and cook rapidly, stirring often to prevent sticking, until the jam reaches the gelling point.

4. Spoon hot jam into prepared jars, leaving ¼ inch head space.

5. Wipe the lip of each jar with a damp paper towel, top the jars with a lid and a lid ring.

6. Process the jars in a water bath canner for 15 minutes. Remove and let cool completely.

Makes about 8 half-pints.

Raspberry-Blueberry Jam

When I was a child, our next-door neighbor grew raspberries and blackberries.

The bushes, as berries are wont to do, multiplied and escaped his yard, taking up residence in ours. Some people may have found this annoying, but my family was thrilled.

There were big red and yellow raspberries and juicy blackberries. My mother sent us out every summer to pick them for jam. We didn't rebel, mostly because we ate as many as we picked and came in with red and purple stained fingers.

When my own children were young we visited abandoned farm fields in Maine, picking pails of the berries that had sprouted up wherever they had the space.

We moved west and I did three things the first few weeks; got a library card, planted a peach tree, and planted several raspberry bushes. Now we are on the fourth generation of raspberry lovers. Both of my sons have raspberries growing in their own yards, and their children share red stained fingers too.

INGREDIENTS

- 4 ½ CUPS FRESH RASPBERRIES
- 4 ½ CUPS FRESH BLUEBERRIES
- 6 CUPS GRANULATED SUGAR

1. Add the raspberries, blueberries, and sugar to a large Dutch oven.

2. Slowly bring the mixture to a boil over medium heat stirring until the sugar is dissolved.

3. Turn the heat up a little and cook rapidly, stirring often to prevent sticking, until the jam reaches the gelling point.

4. Spoon hot jam into prepared jars, leaving ¼ inch head space.

5. Wipe the lip of each jar with a damp paper towel, top the jars with a lid and a lid ring.

6. Process the jars in a water bath canner for 15 minutes. Remove and let cool completely.

Makes about 7 half-pints.

Wildberry Jam

Are you familiar with Gifford's Ice Cream? If not, you are missing a treat.

One summer when my children were toddlers, my husband's job took him away from us for 14 days at a time. Believe me, those days were *long* for me and my boys! To help speed the time, we drove down the mountain at least once a week for some creamy Gifford's Ice Cream. The kids usually chose Smurf cones (I can't really remember how they were made but it involved *very* blue ice cream), but I was partial to their Wildberry flavor. It had a little bit of everything in it, along with actual berry chunks.

I had Wildberry in mind when I made this end-of-the-berries jam that uses raspberries, blueberries, blackberries, and strawberries. If you can't find Gifford's Wildberry Ice Cream, the next best thing might be a scoop of good old vanilla topped with this homemade jam.

> **Fun Fact:** *Tiny wild blueberries are packed with intense flavor. They primarily grow in Eastern Maine and Nova Scotia. Cherryfield, Maine is the self-proclaimed "blueberry capital of the world".*

Ingredients

- 3 CUPS HALVED STRAWBERRIES
- 3 CUPS BLUEBERRIES
- 2 CUPS BLACKBERRIES
- 2 CUPS RED RASPBERRIES
- 6 CUPS GRANULATED SUGAR

1. Add strawberries, blueberries, blackberries, raspberries, and sugar to a large Dutch oven.
2. Slightly crush with a potato masher.
3. Slowly bring the mixture to a boil over medium heat stirring until the sugar is dissolved.
4. Turn the heat up a little and cook rapidly, stirring often to prevent sticking, until the jam reaches the gelling point.
5. Spoon hot jam into prepared jars, leaving ¼ inch head space.
6. Wipe the lip of each jar with a damp paper towel, top the jars with a lid and a lid ring.
7. Process the jars in a water bath canner for 15 minutes. Remove and let cool completely.

Makes about 9 half-pints.

Peach Melba Jam

Sliced peaches, vanilla ice cream and raspberry puree. Sounds delicious, doesn't it?

When a dessert has been around for over 100 years you know it has to be good. Peach Melba fits this category. It is simple but elegant; a dessert we can serve to family but equally welcomed by guests.

The famous chef, Auguste Escoffier, invented Peach Melba in honor of opera singer Nellie Melba. The original version included vanilla ice cream with sliced fresh peaches and spun sugar. Later M. Escoffier updated his famous recipe and added raspberry sauce to the ice cream and peaches.

Sometimes though, we don't have access to sliced peaches and raspberry puree. The season for both fruits is short after all. In that situation Peach Melba Jam comes to the rescue.

Spoon this jam over a scoop of ice cream or pound cake. Sprinkle with chopped almonds or top with whipped cream. Light and easy. The best kind of dessert.

INGREDIENTS

- 5 CUPS DICED PEACHES
- 3 CUP RASPBERRIES
- ½ CUP WATER
- 6 CUPS GRANULATED SUGAR

1. Add peaches, raspberries, water and sugar to a large Dutch oven.

2. Slowly bring the mixture to a boil over medium heat stirring until the sugar is dissolved.

3. Turn the heat up a little and cook rapidly, stirring often to prevent sticking, until the jam reaches the gelling point.

4. Spoon hot jam into prepared jars, leaving ¼ inch head space.

5. Wipe the lip of each jar with a damp paper towel, top the jars with a lid and a lid ring.

6. Process the jars in a water bath canner for 15 minutes. Remove and let cool completely.

Makes about 8 half-pints.

Apricot Amaretto Jam

I started experimenting with flavored jams a few years ago, after exhausting local fruit combination jams. I was looking for something that would enhance but not overpower the fruit flavor.

A trip to the liquor store with all those little bottles of spirits convinced me to combine fruit and spirits. Here, almond flavored Amaretto pairs perfectly with sweet-tart apricots. Better yet, most of the alcohol evaporates during the cooking process.

So why use alcohol-based spirits at all? Because certain flavor compounds dissolve in alcohol better than in any other solution. This gives us an intense flavor that can't be found anywhere else.

INGREDIENTS

- 1 2/3 CUPS DICED APRICOTS
- 2 TSP LEMON JUICE
- 1 1/4 CUPS GRANULATED SUGAR
- 1/4 CUP AMARETTO

1. Add apricots, lemon juice, and sugar to a large Dutch oven.
2. Slightly crush the fruit with a potato masher.

3. Slowly bring the mixture to a boil over medium heat stirring until the sugar is dissolved and add the Amaretto.

4. Turn the heat up a little and cook rapidly, stirring often to prevent sticking, until the jam reaches the gelling point.

5. Spoon hot jam into prepared jars, leaving ¼ inch head space.

6. Wipe the lip of each jar with a damp paper towel, top the jars with a lid and a lid ring.

7. Process the jars in a water bath canner for 15 minutes. Remove and let cool completely.

Makes about 2 half-pints.

Raspberry-Blueberry-Mulberry Jam

It was so exciting when my son and his family moved into a house with a backyard mulberry tree. Well…. it was exciting for me. Probably not so much for them. You see, mulberries are messy.

Mulberries are purple berries that look somewhat like blackberries, only they grow on a tree instead of a bush. Birds love mulberries above all else, turning a lone mulberry tree into a cackling mess.

Luckily one year my grand-daughter braved the birds and collected a few mulberries. We made this yummy jam, which is similar to the Raspberry-Blueberry Jam and the Wildberry Jam, but has a unique tartness.

Planting your own mulberry tree may cause your yard to turn purple with dropped berries, but it also keeps the birds away from your other fruit trees. Hundreds of birds will take up residence in the mulberry tree, ignoring the luscious fruit on your peach, apricot, cherry or plum trees.

INGREDIENTS
- 4 CUPS RASPBERRIES
- 4 CUPS BLUEBERRIES
- 1 CUP MULBERRIES
- 6 CUPS GRANULATED SUGAR

1. Add raspberries, blueberries, mulberries, and sugar to a large Dutch oven.

2. Slowly bring the mixture to a boil over medium heat stirring until the sugar is dissolved.

3. Turn the heat up a little and cook rapidly, stirring often to prevent sticking, until the jam reaches the gelling point.

4. Spoon hot jam into prepared jars, leaving ¼ inch head space.

5. Wipe the lip of each jar with a damp paper towel, top the jars with a lid and a lid ring.

6. Process the jars in a water bath canner for 15 minutes. Remove and let cool completely.

Makes about 8 half-pints.

Spiced Apple Maple Jam

Canning is a year-round activity in my house. When I saw a similar recipe in the *100th Anniversary edition of the Ball Blue Book*, I knew I had to adapt it to my own tastes with some ingredient changes.

I wasn't disappointed. This jam would be good on pancakes or served as a glaze for pork chops, chicken breasts, or meat analogs. My family loves it with that old stand-by, peanut butter. Bonus – the recipe is easy to prepare and makes quite a lot, about 8 half-pints.

For best results and complex flavor, use at least 2 different apple varieties. Combine a sweeter apple like a Golden Delicious, Gala, or Fuji with a tart apple like Braeburn, Granny Smith, or Empire.

INGREDIENTS

- 6 LBS. APPLES
- 6 CUPS OF GRANULATED SUGAR
- 1 TSP GROUND CINNAMON
- ½ TSP GROUND ALLSPICE
- ¼ TSP GROUND MACE
- ¼ TSP GROUND CLOVES
- 1 CUP MAPLE SYRUP (BE SURE TO USE REAL MAPLE SYRUP, NOT MAPLE-FLAVORED SYRUP)

1. Peel, core and chop the apples. Add the apples, sugar, spices and maple syrup to a large Dutch oven.

2. Slowly bring the mixture to a boil over medium heat stirring often to prevent sticking, about 40 minutes.

3. Turn the heat up a little and cook rapidly, until the jam reaches the gelling point.

4. Spoon hot jam into prepared jars, leaving ¼ inch head space.

5. Wipe the lip of each jar with a damp paper towel, top the jars with a lid and a lid ring.

6. Process the jars in a water bath canner for 15 minutes. Remove and let cool completely.

Makes about 8 half-pints.

Fig Jam with Anise

Nothing can compare to ripe, juicy, fresh figs. Soft to the bite, rich in flavor. Similar to a date, but less heavy.

Figs are native to the Mediterranean region, and even grow in several places in the U.S. Sadly, they do not grow near my home in the Mid-Columbia. Our winters are too cold for a poor fig tree to survive. So I limit my fresh fig tastings to rare trips to the Portland, Oregon farmer's market where I indulge with abandon.

Except sometimes fresh figs show up in the local grocery store. They are usually wrapped in plastic and over-ripe by the time they get here, but I buy them nonetheless.

Recently I purchased a few containers of both black Mission figs and green Calimyrna figs. Some of the figs were perfect for eating out of hand, but most were past their prime. No problem. I reached for one of my favorite canning books, **The Joy of Jams, Jellies, and Other Sweet Preserves** by Linda Ziedrich, adapted her recipe, and turned my too-soft figs into a fantastic chunky jam with just a hint of flavor-enhancing anise.

INGREDIENTS

- 2 LBS CHOPPED FRESH FIGS
- ½ CUP WATER
- 3 CUPS GRANULATED SUGAR
- ½ TSP ANISE SEED
- 2 TBSP LEMON JUICE

1. Add figs, water, sugar, anise seed, and lemon juice to a large Dutch oven.

2. Slowly bring the mixture to a boil over medium heat stirring until the sugar is dissolved.

3. Boil gently, stirring often, for 10-15 minutes or until thickened.

4. Spoon the hot jam into prepared jars, leaving ¼ inch head space.

5. Wipe the lip of each jar with a damp paper towel, top the jars with a lid and a lid ring.

6. Process the jars in a water bath canner for 10 minutes. Remove and let cool completely.

Makes about 5 half-pints.

Rose Petal Jam

Do you ever feel that you were born in the wrong century? That you have an appreciation for simple times, simple tastes and handcrafted items that just isn't common today? Me too. Whether it's due to ancestral memory, reincarnation, or just the result of reading too many historical novels, I feel a connection to the past that goes way beyond filling in genealogy charts. Rose petal jam is one of those days gone by concoctions that your great-grandmother might remember.

It only takes a few minutes to pick the rose petals and then this recipe is quick and easy to prepare. In the end you will have a unique jam that makes a perfect gift. Some observations:

- The whole house smells wonderful while the jam is cooking. In fact, the rose smell lingers for a few days but it isn't overpowering. Use red or dark pink roses as they are the most flavorful. I also used some dark orange roses.

- Trim the white bitter part at the base of the petals before using.

- Some people make this jam as a syrup and petal combination. I reduced the petals to more of a traditional jam consistency.

- Rose Petal Jam would be great spread on biscuits for afternoon tea or made into an unusual jam tart. Or tucked into butter cookies, or rolled in phyllo, or served along with grilled chicken.

- Note that since the jam processing time is only 5 minutes, jars must be sterilized first.

INGREDIENTS

- 12 CUPS RED OR PINK ROSE PETALS
- 4 CUPS GRANULATED SUGAR
- 2 TSP LEMON JUICE

1. Gather rose petals in the morning, after dew has dried but before the heat of the day. Rinse in a bowl of water and drain.

2. Sprinkle petals with sugar and knead with your fingers, breaking up the rose petals as you knead. Cover and refrigerate for at least 2 hours.

3. Add rose mixture and lemon juice to a large saucepan and heat over low heat for 10 minutes, stirring constantly. At this point, you can pulverize the mixture in a food processor or blender to achieve more of a traditional jam texture, if desired.

4. Continue cooking over medium heat for 5 - 10 more minutes or until a thick syrup has formed.

5. Add jam to sterilized jars, cover with two-piece caps, and process in a water bath canner for 5 minutes.

Makes 4 half-pint jars.

Cranberry Christmas Jam

Summer isn't the only time of the year to make jam. This Christmas jam uses the best of autumn's harvest – cranberries and apples.

Cranberries, full of healthy antioxidants, add a fresh, tart flavor to breads and sauces. Their flavor melds especially well with apples and warm spices.

This spicy jam is delicious spread on homemade biscuits or post-holiday turkey sandwiches. It also makes an interesting fill for Christmas cookies.

> ***Fun Fact****: Cranberries, blueberries, and Concord grapes are the only Native American berries grown commercially.*

INGREDIENTS

- 1 (12OZ.) PKG CRANBERRIES, ABOUT 3 CUPS
- 6 CUPS PEELED, DICED APPLES
- 1 ¾ CUPS WATER
- 6 CUPS GRANULATED SUGAR
- ½ TSP GROUND ALLSPICE
- ½ TSP GROUND CINNAMON
- ¼ TSP GROUND CLOVES

1. Add the cranberries, apples, water, sugar, and spices to a large Dutch oven.

2. Slowly bring the mixture to a boil over medium heat stirring until the sugar is dissolved.

3. Turn the heat up a little and cook rapidly, stirring often to prevent sticking, until the jam reaches the gelling point.

4. Use the plate method to check for gelling or use a digital thermometer. Gelling is reached at 220 degrees or 8 degrees above the boiling point of water.

5. Spoon the hot jam into prepared jars, leaving ¼ inch head space.

6. Wipe the lip of each jar with a damp paper towel, top the jars with a lid and a lid ring.

7. Process the jars in a water bath canner for 15 minutes. Remove and let cool completely.

Makes about 6 half-pints.

Cherry-Lime Jam

One year our sweet cherry tree was overladen with cherries. Miraculously we were able to harvest them before the birds and bugs got their fill.

I pitted and froze bags and bags of cherries. My fingers were purple for days. I cooked with cherries until the family begged me to stop. Apparently not everyone is crazy about cherries.

So, I made jam. Cherries and lime are excellent flavor partners. Lime's tartness cuts cherry's sweetness, enhancing the flavor of both.

The texture here is similar to a marmalade or preserve. It is a bit more of a syrup and fruit combination than most jam recipes.

INGREDIENTS

- 4 CUPS PITTED SWEET CHERRIES
- 4 CUPS GRANULATED SUGAR
- JUICE FROM 2 LIMES, APPROX. ¼ CUP
- ¼ CUP WATER
- ZEST FROM 2 LIMES

1. Add the cherries, sugar, lime juice and water to a large Dutch oven.
2. Slowly bring the mixture to a boil over medium heat stirring until the sugar is dissolved.

3. Turn the heat up a little and cook rapidly, stirring often to prevent sticking, until the jam reaches the gelling point, about 35 minutes.

4. Add the lime zest, stirring to evenly distribute throughout the jam.

5. Use the plate method to check for gelling or use a digital thermometer. Gelling is reached at 220 degrees or 8 degrees above the boiling point of water.

6. Spoon hot jam into prepared jars, leaving ¼ inch head space.

7. Wipe the lip of each jar with a damp paper towel, top the jars with a lid and a lid ring.

8. Process the jars in a water bath canner for 15 minutes. Remove and let cool completely.

Makes about 5 half-pints.

Blackberry Maple Jam

Blackberries are considered a nuisance in many places. Something that grows abundantly and takes over any bare patch of ground, leaving purple-black sticky stains everywhere. I remember buying quarts of freshly picked blackberries from the neighborhood children who saw picking the ubiquitous berries as an easier lemonade stand alternative.

How things change with location! Now I live in an arid environment that isn't quite as friendly to blackberries. I purchase little four-ounce trays instead of quarts. And they cost lots more! After years of this I finally put in a few backyard bushes. Hopefully there will be some to harvest this year.

This recipe combines two well-known New England flavors; black berries and maple. Since both are prolific in the Northeast, it only makes sense to pair them.

INGREDIENTS
- 4 CUPS BLACKBERRIES
- 1 ⅓ CUPS GRANULATED SUGAR
- 1 ⅓ CUPS MAPLE SYRUP

1. Add blackberries, sugar, and maple syrup to a large Dutch oven.
2. Mash some of the berries with a potato masher.

3. Slowly bring the mixture to a boil over medium heat stirring until the sugar is dissolved.

4. Turn the heat up a little and cook rapidly, stirring often to prevent sticking, until the jam reaches the gelling point.

5. Spoon hot jam into prepared jars, leaving ¼ inch head space.

6. Wipe the lip of each jar with a damp paper towel, top the jars with a lid and a lid ring.

7. Process the jars in a water bath canner for 15 minutes. Remove and let cool completely.

Makes about 3 half-pints.

CHAPTER FOUR
Fruit Butter Recipes

If you are nervous about making jams or preserves, fruit butters are an excellent introduction to sweet spreads. You don't have to worry about determining the gelling point or over cooking the fruit-sugar concoction when making fruit butters.

Fruit butters are simply made by cooking, pureeing, and reducing fruit and sugar to a thickened spread, similar to a thick applesauce. Fruit butters also have less sugar than most fruit spreads.

Tip: When making fruit butters use ½ as much sugar per batch as fruit puree. For example; if you have 8 cups of puree add 4 cups of sugar. 6 cups of puree require 3 cups of sugar, 2 cups of puree need 1 cup of sugar, and so on.

Peach Butter

During the harvest season, our Red Haven Peach tree is often overladen with ripe peaches. There are so many peaches I have trouble picking them before the very well-fed neighborhood squirrel gets more than his fair share.

Most of the first picking goes into the freezer, but I also make peach butter. Unlike jams and preserves, butters are cooked slowly for a long period of time. Butters are pretty easy to make and it's difficult to screw up a batch, but they are a little time consuming.

Although you may be most familiar with apple butter, fruit butter can be made from almost any fruit. I've made blueberry butter, plum butter, cherry butter, and apricot butter. Since our eldest grand-daughter prefers peach butter to all others, I make sure we have several jars in the cupboard.

INGREDIENTS

- 18–20 MEDIUM–SIZED RIPE PEACHES
- 4 CUPS GRANULATED SUGAR

1. Peel and slice the peaches.
2. Place in a large pot and cook over low heat until soft, adding small amounts of water if necessary to prevent scorching.
3. Puree peaches in a blender or food processor or using an immersion blender.

4. Measure puree.

5. Return puree to pot - you should have about 8 cups of puree. Add sugar.

6. Cook over medium-low heat, stirring often until mixture has thickened.

7. Ladle into hot, clean jars leaving about ¼ inch head space. Top with the two-piece lids and rings, and process in a water bath for 10 minutes.

Makes about 8 half-pints.

Spiced Pear Butter

It's only recently, in my soon-to-be *golden years*, that I have developed an appreciation for pears.

It turns out that pears are an excellent choice for the things that ail us. They have lots of soluble fiber and thus work to lower cholesterol. They are a good choice for gall bladder support for the same reason. Plus, they are picked before ripe and ripen on the counter – so they are ready to eat when we are ready to eat them.

Like apples, pears combine well with autumn's warm spices. Serve this pear butter spread on pork chops or topping homemade gingerbread.

INGREDIENTS

- 18 – 20 RIPE PEARS
- ABOUT 4 CUPS GRANULATED SUGAR
- 1 ½ TSP GROUND GINGER
- ¼ TSP GROUND CLOVES

1. Peel, core, and slice the pears.
2. Place in a large pot and cook over low heat until soft, adding small amounts of water if necessary to prevent scorching.
3. Puree pears in a blender or food processor or using an immersion blender.
4. Measure puree.

5. Return puree to pot - you should have about 8 cups of puree. Add sugar and spices.

6. Cook over medium-low heat, stirring often until mixture has thickened.

7. Ladle into hot, clean jars leaving about ¼ inch head space. Top with the two-piece lids and rings, and process in a water bath for 10 minutes.

Makes about 8 half-pints.

Butternut Squash Butter

As a native New Englander, I have been eating winter squash my whole life. Not many vegetables grow well in northern Maine, but winter squash seems to love the weather. Thus, we grow up eating winter squash mashed with butter, roasted, pureed or chopped for soup, stuffed with rice, and turned into pie. But I don't ever remember eating squash butter until recently – and even then, it wasn't squash. It was a yummy maple pumpkin butter I had while on vacation in Bar Harbor, Maine.

After returning home I cleaned out the garden and set aside some of the butternut squash. This version of squash butter turned out the best. Since butternut squash has a more delicate flavor than pumpkin, I used honey instead of maple syrup.

The spices have also been tweaked; with less cinnamon than most pumpkin butter recipes plus the addition of mace. The whole thing was brightened with orange zest and fresh orange juice.

If you can refrain from eating the butter from the jar with a spoon, it is good spread on a ham sandwich, topping a freshly baked scone, or tucked into cake filling.

Squash and pumpkin butter cannot be safely canned at home. Place jars of the butter in the freezer for future use. And be sure to add the zest after the butter is all done cooking. Adding the zest while cooking will make the butter bitter.

INGREDIENTS

- 3 CUPS COOKED, PUREED BUTTERNUT SQUASH
- 1 ½ CUPS MILD HONEY
- ZEST FROM 1 LARGE ORANGE
- JUICE FROM 1 LARGE ORANGE
- ½ TSP GROUND CINNAMON
- ½ TSP GROUND ALLSPICE
- ½ TSP GROUND GINGER
- ¼ TSP GROUND MACE

1. Add all ingredients except orange zest to a large saucepan.
2. Bring mixture to a boil.
3. Reduce heat and cook until smooth and thick.
4. Stir in orange zest.
5. Fill ½ pint canning jars.
6. Refrigerate for up to a month, or store in freezer.

Makes about 4 half-pints.

Rose Hip Apple Butter

I am living proof that you can take the girl out of the Northeast, but it's pretty difficult to take the thrifty Yankee out of the girl. In my house, left-over mashed potatoes become enchiladas, worn out towels are turned into pot holders, and beautiful, nutritious food – free for the taking – becomes jam.

Wild rose hips, also known as beach rose hips, are an excellent source of vitamin C. They also have a lovely, fresh floral aroma and a tangy taste that jumps off the tongue. And they are prolific in my front yard. I don't mind sharing them with the birds, but I turn my share into jam.

When picking rose hips there are a couple of things to keep in mind:

- Use only the hips from wild roses (rosa rugosa).

- Only use hips that have not been sprayed with insecticides.

- Hips are easier to peel after they have been through a frost. Mother Nature preserves the hips right on the bush until you are ready to use them.

- Be prepared to get stuck by thorns when picking the rose hips.

INGREDIENTS

- 12 CUPS ROSE HIPS
- 6 LARGE APPLES
- 1 ½ CUPS WATER
- 4 CUPS GRANULATED SUGAR
- 2 TBSP LEMON JUICE
- ⅛ TSP EACH GROUND MACE AND GROUND CLOVES

1. Wash the hips, trim the ends, and peel. There are two methods to peel the hips: Pull off the skin and as much pulp as possible without breaking through into the seeds. Or cut the hips open and scrape out the seeds. I got about 2 cups of skin and pulp.

2. Wash, core and slice the apples.

3. Combine the apples, rose hips, and water in a large sauce pot. Cook until apples are soft.

4. Remove from the heat and puree. I got about 6 cups of ruby red puree.

5. Return the puree to the sauce pot. Add sugar, lemon juice and spices.

6. Cook until the mixture thickens, about 20 minutes.

7. Ladle into hot, clean jars leaving about ¼ inch head space. Top with the two-piece lids and rings, and process in a water bath for 10 minutes.

Makes about 7 half-pints.

Spiced Peach Butter

How to Peel Peaches

Most directions tell you to scald the peaches first and the skins will slip off but that has never been my experience. I find it's just as easy, and a lot less work, to peel the peaches with a paring knife and forgo the scalding. However, some peach varieties do respond well to the scalding method. Drop the peaches into boiling water for about 30 seconds. Remove and immediately plunge them into ice water. Drain and voila, the skins can be easily removed. If you are lucky!

How Long Should You Cook Peach Butter?

It's really important to keep stirring the puree/sugar mixture as it will burn very easily. While peach butter is a wonderful thing, burned peach butter is a frustrating waste of time and money – I've made this mistake so you don't have to. Constant stirring isn't necessary but frequent stirring will lead to better results.

As the butter thickens it will become a deep, rich, orange-yellow color. This process takes anywhere from 30 minutes to an hour or more.

INGREDIENTS

- 18–20 MEDIUM–SIZED RIPE PEACHES
- 4 CUPS GRANULATED SUGAR
- 1 TSP GROUND ALLSPICE
- 1 TSP GROUND GINGER

1. Peel and slice the peaches.

2. Place in a large pot and cook over low heat until soft, adding small amounts of water if necessary to prevent scorching.

3. Puree peaches in a blender or food processor or using an immersion blender.

4. Return puree to pot - you should have about 8 cups of puree. Add sugar and spices.

5. Cook over medium-low heat, stirring often until mixture has thickened.

6. Ladle into hot, clean jars leaving about ¼ inch head space. Top with the two-piece lids and rings, and process in a water bath for 15 minutes.

Makes about 8 half-pints.

Brown Sugar Bourbon Peach Butter

This recipe was another experiment from my liquor store inspiration – see Apricot Amaretto Jam.

Although we often think of peach as a light, summery flavor, peach and caramel flavors meld well too.

Here I expanded on that flavor palate by using brown sugar and bourbon. Once again, the alcohol burns off while cooking, leaving bourbon's caramel notes behind.

INGREDIENTS

- 4–5 LARGE PEACHES
- 1 CUP PACKED BROWN SUGAR
- ¼ CUP BOURBON

1. Peel and slice peaches.
2. Place in a large pot and cook over low heat until soft, adding small amounts of water if necessary to prevent scorching.
3. Puree peaches in a blender or food processor or using an immersion blender.
4. Measure puree.
5. Return puree to pot - you should have about 2 cups of puree. Add sugar and bourbon.

6. Cook over medium-low heat, stirring often until mixture has thickened.

7. Ladle into hot, clean jars leaving about ¼ inch head space. Top with the two-piece lids and rings, and process in a water bath for 10 minutes.

Makes about 2 half-pints.

Spirited Apricot Cherry Butter

This recipe was my favorite "liquor store" experiment. I just love the tart apricot and sweet cherry combination with Grand Marnier's orange richness.

Grand Marnier is an orange flavored Cognac similar to Cointreau. The difference, as far as I can determine, is that Grand Marnier is aged – as a good Cognac should be! - while Cointreau and other Triple Sec liqueurs are not aged.

To my taste, Grand Marnier lends a fuller, richer flavor than Cointreau; one that balances the lighter apricot and cherry flavors.

INGREDIENTS
- 10 LARGE APRICOTS
- 1 CUP SWEET CHERRIES, PITTED
- 2 ¼ CUP GRANULATED SUGAR
- ¼ CUP GRAND MARNIER

1. Chop apricots. Place in a large pot with the cherries and cook over low heat until soft, adding small amounts of water if necessary to prevent scorching.
2. Puree fruit in a blender or food processor or using an immersion blender.
3. Measure puree.

4. Return puree to pot - you should have about 4 ½ cups of puree. Add sugar and Grand Marnier.

5. Cook over medium-low heat, stirring often until mixture has thickened.

6. Ladle into hot, clean jars leaving about ¼ inch head space. Top with the two-piece lids and rings, and process in a water bath for 10 minutes.

Makes 4 half-pints.

Rum Apple Butter

Apples have a little secret, one that most people notice but that seldom gets mentioned. The secret? When cooked, apples lose their distinctive flavor and meld into everything else.

If you can think of something with a strong apple taste, it was probably made with artificial flavoring – which isn't apple at all.

The trick is to combine apple with something that will enhance its flavor but not overpower it. Here we use rum for this purpose. Calvados or another apple brandy would work well too.

The alcohol is cooked out while the rum flavor remains, turning this apple butter into a special treat. Spread it on toasted English muffins, use as a filling for spice cake, or serve with pork chops.

INGREDIENTS

- 2 LBS APPLES (USE AT LEAST TWO DIFFERENT VARIETIES OF APPLES FOR INCREASED FLAVOR)
- ½ CUP WATER
- ½ CUP DARK RUM
- 2 CUPS GRANULATED SUGAR
- 1 TSP GROUND CINNAMON
- ¼ TSP GROUND CLOVES

1. Wash apples. Core but do not peel. Cut into small pieces.

2. Place in a large pot with water and rum. Cook over low heat until soft.

3. Puree apples and liquid in a blender or food processor or using an immersion blender.

4. Measure puree.

5. Return puree to pot - you should have about 4 cups of puree. Add sugar and spices.

6. Cook over medium-low heat, stirring often until mixture has thickened.

7. Ladle into hot, clean jars leaving about ¼ inch head space. Top with the two-piece lids and rings, and process in a water bath for 10 minutes.

Makes about 5 half-pints.

Spiced Apricot Plum Butter

Some years, if the weather has cooperated and the planets are aligned, the late apricots and early plums arrive at the Farmer's Market simultaneously. When that happens, I make this spiced butter treat.

Use black or red plums here and you will have a beautiful pink spread. Spiced apricot plum butter made with yellow plums will still taste amazing, but will not be as pleasing to the eye. This is because the cinnamon turns the yellow puree a rather dun color.

INGREDIENTS

- 1 LB PLUMS
- 2 ½ LBS APRICOTS
- 4 CUPS GRANULATED SUGAR
- 1 TSP GROUND GINGER
- ½ TSP GROUND CINNAMON

1. Wash and chop the plums and apricots.
2. Place in a large pot and cook over low heat until soft, adding small amounts of water if necessary to prevent scorching.
3. Puree fruit in a blender or food processor or using an immersion blender.
4. Measure puree.

5. Return puree to pot - you should have about 8 cups of puree. Add sugar and spices.

6. Cook over medium-low heat, stirring often until mixture has thickened.

7. Ladle into hot, clean jars leaving about ¼ inch head space. Top with the two-piece lids and rings, and process in a water bath for 10 minutes.

Makes about 8 half-pints.

Sweet Cherry Almond Butter

It's funny how some years Mother Nature bestows us with an abundance of one crop or another, only to snatch it back the very next year and leave us with dregs.

That has been the story of our cherry tree experiment. After planting and nurturing, waiting for maturity, and gratefully harvesting a few cherries each year, we had a year of "Oh my goodness! I am drowning in cherries!"

That watershed year led to all kinds of new cherry concoctions in my recipe file, including this Cherry Almond Butter.

INGREDIENTS

- 3-4 LBS SWEET CHERRIES, PITTED
- 3 CUPS GRANULATED SUGAR
- 1 TSP ALMOND EXTRACT

1. Place pitted cherries in a large pot and cook over low heat until soft, adding small amounts of water if necessary to prevent scorching.
2. Puree cooked cherries in a blender or food processor or using an immersion blender.
3. Measure puree.
4. Return puree to pot - you should have about 6 cups of puree. Add sugar.

5. Cook over medium-low heat, stirring often until mixture has thickened. Add almond extract, stirring to evenly distribute.

6. Ladle into hot, clean jars leaving about ¼ inch head space. Top with the two-piece lids and rings, and process in a water bath for 10 minutes.

Makes about 4 half-pints.

Port Wine Plum Butter

I love fruit butters because they allow for a little more creativity than many soft spreads. I've made several different combinations in the past like rose hip-apple butter and cherry-almond butter, but my favorite has always been ripe, delicious peach butter. Until now.

This port-wine plum butter is my new favorite. Tart plums are enhanced by the port-wine's deep, rich flavor. You can't actually taste the port-wine, it just increases the plum notes. When you read about a wine have flavors of plums and blackberries, this is the same thing, only our plums have flavors of wine rather than wine having flavors of plum.

INGREDIENTS

- 2 – 3 LBS PLUMS
- 2 ½ CUPS GRANULATED SUGAR
- ¼ CUP PORT WINE

1. Chop plums, removing pits.
2. Add plums to a large Dutch oven or other pot and cook over medium-low heat until soft. Add tiny amounts of water to keep plums from sticking or burning to the pan if necessary.
3. Puree cooked plums using a blender, food processor, or immersion blender. You should have

about 5 cups of puree. Return puree to pot and add sugar and port wine.

4. Cook over medium-low heat, stirring often to prevent scorching.

5. The butter will thicken as it cooks This process takes anywhere from 30 minutes to an hour or more.

6. Cook until the butter is thick enough to round up on a spoon, or as thick as you prefer.

7. Ladle into hot, clean ½ pint jars leaving about ¼ inch head space. Top with the two-piece lids and rings, and process in a water bath for 15 minutes.

Makes about 4 half-pints.

.

Rose Hip Mango Butter

My goal in life is to live someplace where I can grow a mango tree. I love mango's sweet flavor and its almost citrus-like over notes.

Most years mango and rose hips are not available at the same time. But one year was chilly enough to keep the rose hips refrigerated by nature until mangoes showed up in the grocery aisle.

The two fruits are an excellent sweet-sour combination. The resulting butter is a beautiful persimmon hue. You could use frozen mango here too.

INGREDIENTS

- 15 CUPS ROSE HIPS •
- 5 LARGE MANGOES OR 6 CUPS CHOPPED MANGO
- ⅔ CUP LEMON JUICE
- 2 ¾ CUP GRANULATED SUGAR

1. Remove the skin and pulp from the rose hips either by running through a food mill or by hand.
2. Place rose hips and chopped mango in a large pot and cook over low heat until soft, adding small amounts of water if necessary to prevent scorching.

3. Puree fruit in a blender or food processor or using an immersion blender.

4. Measure puree.

5. Return puree to pot - you should have about 5 ½ cups of puree. Add lemon juice and sugar.

6. Cook over medium-low heat, stirring often until mixture has thickened.

7. Ladle into hot, clean jars leaving about ¼ inch head space. Top with the two-piece lids and rings, and process in a water bath for 10 minutes.

Makes about 7 half-pints.

CHAPTER FIVE
Preserves Recipes

At first glance, preserves and jams seem to be the same thing. The difference is in how they are prepared before cooking. Although it may seem to be a slight difference, the resulting flavors and textures are quite dissimilar.

Jams are prepared by chopping or crushing the fruit, mixing it with sugar, and cooking to a gel.

Preserves are made by chopping the fruit, mixing it with sugar, and *allowing it to macerate* before cooking.

When jam cooks, the fruit breaks down. You usually can't pick out individual pieces of fruit in jam, because it has all broken down while cooking.

Macerating the fruit in preserves lets the individual pieces mostly retain their shape while cooking. So, a preserve is less a *jammy muddle* and more a *concoction of fruit pieces* suspended in thickened syrup.

Peach Preserves

I much prefer preserves over jam. Some people will tell you that there is no taste difference but they are wrong! To me, preserves have a fresher fruit taste compared to jam or jelly.

I've been following this particular recipe so long I could make it in my sleep. But the whole family looks forward to receiving peach preserves at Christmas, and the grandchildren love it year-round.

The difference between preserves and jam? In preserves the fruit is "preserved" with the sugar and thus holds its shape while cooking. Most preserves combine fruit and sugar, and then sit for a while. The cooking process is slow. You will have better luck following the plate method to check gelling than the temperature method when making preserves.

Jam is made from crushed or chopped fruit and is cooked quickly after the sugar melts. Both should be made in small batches.

INGREDIENTS

- 8 CUPS PEELED, SLICED PEACHES (ABOUT 10 LARGE PEACHES).
- 6 CUPS OF GRANULATED SUGAR

1. Combine peaches and sugar in a large bowl.

2. Cover and let sit in the refrigerator for 12-18 hours.

3. Transfer the fruit/sugar combination to a large saucepan.

4. Bring slowly to a boil over medium heat. Stir frequently to prevent scorching.

5. Boil gently until the fruit becomes clear and the syrup thickens, about 40 minutes.

6. Use the plate method to check for gelling or use a digital thermometer. Gelling is reached at 220 degrees or 8 degrees above the boiling point of water.

7. Spoon the hot preserves into prepared jars, leaving ¼ inch head space.

8. Wipe the lip of each jar with a damp paper towel, top the jars with a lid and a lid ring.

9. Process the jars in a water bath canner for 15 minutes. Remove and let cool completely.

Makes about 7 half-pints.

Cherry Preserves

We grow many varieties of sweet cherries here in the Mid-Columbia, but not many sour cherries. So, when I found fresh sour (or pie) cherries at the Farmer's Market, I quickly purchased three pounds for my favorite preserves – sour cherry.

I find that this particular mixture produces a lot of foam while cooking. Most recipes tell you to skim off the foam and dispose of it. I guess I am too lazy to do that. Instead, when the syrup is thickened, remove the saucepan from the heat and stir the preserves until the foam is completely collapsed, then continue to ladle into the jars.

INGREDIENTS

- 3 LBS SOUR CHERRIES, PITTED
- 4 ¾ CUPS GRANULATED SUGAR
- 2 TBSP LEMON JUICE

1. Combine cherries and sugar in a large saucepan. Cover and let sit for 1 hour.
2. Bring slowly to a boil over medium heat. Stir frequently to prevent scorching.
3. Increase the heat to medium-high and bring to a full boil, continuing to stir occasionally to prevent sticking and burning.

4. Boil for 5 minutes, remove the saucepan from the heat, cover and let sit for 12-16 hours.

5. Add lemon juice and bring the mixture to a boil over medium heat. Once again, increase the heat to medium-high and continue boiling until the syrup has thickened, about 15-20 minutes.

6. Use the plate method to check for gelling or use a digital thermometer. Gelling is reached at 220 degrees or 8 degrees above the boiling point of water.

7. Spoon the hot preserves into prepared jars, leaving ¼ inch head space.

8. Wipe the lip of each jar with a damp paper towel, top the jars with a lid and a lid ring. Process the jars in a water bath canner for 15 minutes. Remove and let cool completely.

Makes about 5 half-pints.

Honey Peach Preserves

Honey, the original sweetener, adds its own unique flavor to preserves. The result is not quite caramel-like, but richer than preserves made with granulated sugar.

Use a mild flavored honey like orange blossom or wildflower. Buckwheat or another strong honey will overpower the peach flavor.

INGREDIENTS

- 8 CUPS PEELED, SLICED PEACHES (ABOUT 10 LARGE PEACHES)
- 3 CUPS OF GRANULATED SUGAR
- 3 CUPS HONEY

1. Combine peaches, sugar, and honey in a large bowl.
2. Cover and let sit in the refrigerator for 12-18 hours.
3. Transfer the fruit/sweetener combination to a large saucepan.
4. Bring slowly to a boil over medium heat. Stir frequently to prevent scorching.
5. Boil gently until the fruit becomes clear and the syrup thickens, about 40 minutes.

6. Use the plate method to check for gelling or use a digital thermometer. Gelling is reached at 220 degrees or 8 degrees above the boiling point of water.

7. Spoon the hot preserves into prepared jars, leaving ¼ inch head space.

8. Wipe the lip of each jar with a damp paper towel, top the jars with a lid and a lid ring.

9. Process the jars in a water bath canner for 15 minutes. Remove and let cool.

Makes about 7 half-pints.

Plum Preserves

I developed this recipe many years ago after being gifted with a couple of big bags of fresh plums.

It has become such a family favorite that my youngest grand-daughter equated "jam" with Plum Preserves. She was four years old before she realized that sweet spreads come in other flavors too!

INGREDIENTS

- 3 CUPS CHOPPED, PITTED RED OR BLACK PLUMS
- 2 CUPS CHOPPED, PITTED YELLOW OR GREEN PLUMS
- 2 CUPS GRANULATED SUGAR
- 2 CUPS HONEY
- 1 CUP WATER

1. Combine plums, sugar and honey in a large sauce pot.
2. Bring slowly to a boil over medium heat. Stir frequently to prevent scorching.
3. Increase heat and cook rapidly until the fruit becomes clear and the syrup thickens, about 15 minutes.
4. Use the plate method to check for gelling or use a digital thermometer. Gelling is reached at 220

degrees or 8 degrees above the boiling point of water.

5. Spoon the hot preserves into prepared jars, leaving ¼ inch head space.

6. Wipe the lip of each jar with a damp paper towel, top the jars with a lid and a lid ring.

7. Process the jars in a water bath canner for 15 minutes. Remove and let cool completely.

Makes about 5 half-pints.

Blueberry Cointreau Preserves

Looking for an easy holiday appetizer? Spread this beautiful jewel-toned preserve over warmed Brie and serve with crackers.

Cointreau's bright orange flavor makes blueberries sing. Blueberry preserves are unusual enough that they will be a welcome gift, but not so unique that they are avoided as an aberration.

INGREDIENTS

- ½ LB BLUEBERRIES
- 1 CUP GRANULATED SUGAR
- ¼ CUP COINTREAU

1. Combine blueberries and sugar in a large saucepan.

2. Bring slowly to a boil over medium heat. Stir frequently to prevent scorching.

3. Reduce heat and simmer for 5 minutes, remove the saucepan from the heat, cover and let sit for 12-16 hours.

4. Bring the mixture to a boil over medium heat. Continue boiling until the syrup has thickened.

5. Add the Cointreau. Stir to evenly distribute.

6. Use the plate method to check for gelling or use a digital thermometer. Gelling is reached at 220 degrees or 8 degrees above the boiling point of water.

7. Spoon the hot preserves into prepared jars, leaving ¼ inch head space.

8. Wipe the lip of each jar with a damp paper towel, top the jars with a lid and a lid ring.

9. Process the jars in a water bath canner for 15 minutes. Remove and let cool completely.

Makes ¾ pint

Peachy Plum Preserves

Every summer, when the backyard peach trees are in full harvest mode, I make jars of peach preserves. Most years I also make plum preserves for my eldest son, since they are his favorite. Last year I didn't get to them. So I was thrilled to find a box of late season peaches and some plump purple plums (say that three times fast!) at the local farm stand.

The peaches were a little worse for wear, so my preserving methods varied. Some were sliced and frozen, some were turned into jars of peach conserve, and most were eaten out of hand. The remainder I turned into this peachy plum recipe. My eldest grand-daughter says it is her new favorite. She especially likes it with peanut butter on that old stand-by, PB & J.

I must admit, although the rest of the family loves this preserve, it is a little sweet for me. Next time I will try adding several different kinds of plums, some that are tarter than those used here.

INGREDIENTS
- 3 CUPS PEELED, CHOPPED PEACHES
- 5 CUPS CHOPPED TART PLUMS
- 6 CUPS GRANULATED SUGAR

1. Combine the fruit and sugar in a large mixing bowl. Stir to mix well.

2. Cover and let sit at room temperature for 6 hours, or up to 24 hours in the refrigerator.

3. Spoon into a large Dutch oven.

4. Bring slowly to a boil, stirring frequently.

5. Boil gently until the fruit becomes almost clear and the syrup is thick, 40 - 50 minutes, stirring often to prevent sticking.

6. Ladle into clean, ½ pint jars. Cover with two-piece caps.

7. Process in a water bath canner for 15 minutes.

Makes about 8 half-pints.

CHAPTER SIX
Syrup, Jelly, and Conserves Recipes

As we near the end of this book, it's probably time for a confession. I love to make jams, preserves, and fruit butters.

In fact, I make so many sweet spreads that my husband thinks I have a "problem." Oh well, there are worse habits.

Cooking from scratch and preserving food at home is in my blood. I am old enough, and grew up in a suitably rural area, that making your meals at home every night was considered normal.

But it was the weekends and summer vacations spent with my Nana and her sisters that fostered my love of home canning. Nana's canned beans were much better than Del Monte's, and Nana's Russian Bear pickles weren't available in any form on the grocery shelf. Nana's ability to take the mouth-puckering chokecherries growing by the garden and turn them into the best jelly ever lit a fire in me that burns to this day.

So, when my husband suggested that we had plenty of jam, I turned to syrup. After all – cooking is a creative endeavor!

Apple Plum Jelly

Although I make tons of jam, I seldom make jelly. Jam can be made quite well without adding a box of pectin, but jelly is finicky. Since jelly has no solids it needs pectin to set. And not all fruits have enough pectin of their own. Just apples, citrus (peels), grapes, quince, and a few others will set up with their own juice.

I don't like spreads made from boxed pectin, it sets up too firm and the pectin upsets my stomach. But every year I try to make at least a couple jars of jelly with natural pectin.

Making jelly isn't difficult; it just requires patience while waiting for the fruit to release its juice. Commercial juice usually won't work because the pectin is broken down in the pasteurization process and then filtered out.

The amount of juice you get from the fruit will vary based on the particular fruit. Use this rule of thumb:

> *Use ¾ the amount of sugar as you have juice. For example, if you have 3 cups of juice use 2 ¼ cups sugar. If you have 1 cup of juice use ¾ cup sugar.*

Canning jars must be sterilized before making jelly. Products processed at least 10 minutes only require clean canning jars. Jelly is only processed 5 minutes, so the jars must be sterilized. Don't be tempted to process the jelly for 10 minutes, it may break down and lose its gel!

INGREDIENTS
- 2 ½ LBS TART APPLES
- ½ TO 1 LB BLACK OR RED PLUMS
- 3 CUPS WATER
- 2 ¼ CUPS GRANULATED SUGAR

1. Prepare juice: Wash apples. Do not peel or core. Cut apples into wedges. Repeat with the plums.

2. Add apples, plums and water to a large pot. Cover and bring to a boil. Reduce heat and simmer until fruit is soft. Let cool slightly.

3. Strain juice through a damp jelly bag or layers of cheesecloth.

4. Make the Jelly: Measure the juice. You should have about 3 cups of juice.

5. Pour juice into a large pot. Add sugar. Note: The amount of juice may vary. Use ¾ as much sugar as you have of juice.

6. Stir to dissolve sugar.

7. Bring to a boil over high heat, stirring constantly.

8. Cook and stir until jelly has set; usually at 8 degrees above boiling water temperature or about 220 degrees.

9. Or, use the sheet test method to determine if the jelly has set.

10. Remove from heat, skim foam if necessary.

11. Ladle into sterilized jars leaving ¼ inch head space.

12. Process in a water bath canner for 5 minutes.

Makes about 3 half-pints.

Apricot Syrup

When life gives you apricots, make syrup! I started making apricot syrup almost out of desperation.

One year, in my enthusiasm for all things fresh and sweet, I purchased 40 pounds of fresh apricots. Yeah. It's a lot of apricots. Plus, the temperature was in triple digits so I wasn't going to be able to let them sit on the counter for very long.

I canned apricot halves and apricot jam. Made apricot leather and dried apricot pieces. Ate lots and lots of fresh apricots. And still had plenty of apricots, so I made syrup. It's been a family favorite ever since, perfect for topping pancakes, waffles, and ice cream.

INGREDIENTS

- 3 LBS APRICOTS
- 6 CUPS GRANULATED SUGAR
- ¼ CUP LEMON JUICE

1. Cut the apricots into quarters and throw away the pits. There is no need to peel the apricots.
2. In a large saucepan, cook the apricots in a little water until they are soft, then puree using a blender or food processor.
3. Measure puree. You should have about 6 cups of puree.

4. Return puree to the sauce pot. Add sugar and lemon juice.

5. Stir mixture until the sugar melts.

6. Bring mixture to a boil over medium heat, stirring often until it reaches 215 – 218 degrees.

7. Remove from heat, stir and skim off any foam. Pour into jars leaving ½ inch of headroom.

8. Wipe the jar rims with a moistened paper towel and put on the two-piece lids.

9. Process in a water bath canner for 10 minutes.

Makes about 4 pints.

Mango Syrup

I love mangoes, but mango canning recipes are difficult to find. There are plenty of savory recipes, like chutney and salsa, but I wanted something sweet.

The thought of tangy mango syrup on my pancakes all winter appeals to me so I developed this recipe from a tested mango sauce recipe. Mangoes are pretty high in both pectin and acid, making this a quick and easy canning project.

INGREDIENTS

- 4 LARGE, RIPE MANGOES
- 3½ CUPS GRANULATED SUGAR (APPROX.)
- 3 TBSP LIME JUICE

1. Peel and cut up mangoes.
2. In a large saucepan, cook the mangoes in a little water until they are soft, then puree in the blender.
3. Measure the puree (I had 3½ cups of puree) and return to the saucepan. Add an equal amount of sugar and about 3 Tbsp (or one Tbsp per cup of puree) of lime juice.
4. Stir the sugar/mango mixture until the sugar melts.

5. Bring the mixture to a boil, and stir often until it almost reaches the gelling point, about 212-215 degrees. This will happen very quickly, it took me less than 10 minutes. This is because man-goes are naturally full of fiber and adding heat causes those fibers to set (gel) rather quickly.

6. Remove the mixture from heat, stir and skim off the foam. Pour into ½ or 1-pint jars (I used ¾ pint jars but they aren't always easy to find). Leave about ½ inch of headroom.

7. Wipe the jar rims with a moistened paper towel and put on the two-piece lids.

8. Process in a water bath canner for 15 minutes.

Makes about 3 pints.

Rose Syrup

2015 was a challenging garden year here in the Northwest. Drought, heat, and low irrigation water didn't add up to a lush garden. So, I increased my backyard foraging.

The purslane, dandelions, and plantain all grew. The borage flowered and abandoned strawberry plants still produced ripe berries. The roses weren't prolific but the blooms were more fragrant than usual.

Although the best edible roses are Rosa damascena and Rosa rugosa, I have had good luck using grafted tea or floribunda roses. So, you can try just about any kind of rose, but – only use roses that have not been sprayed with pesticides! Red roses will result in the most beautiful syrup, but pink roses work as well.

Use your rose syrup:
- Add to sparkling water
- Make a unique Martini or Daiquiri
- Drizzle over pound cake or ice cream
- Use instead of juice in a cake or cookie recipe
- Make homemade rose ice cream
- Spoon over cut watermelon or peaches
- Use in homemade candies

INGREDIENTS

- 6 CUPS ROSE PETALS
- 3 ½ CUPS WATER
- ABOUT 2 ¾ CUPS GRANULATED SUGAR

1. Combine rose petals and water in a large saucepan. Heat to medium, submerging petals when the water is hot.

2. Bring to a boil, reduce heat and simmer for 15 minutes.

3. Strain through a jelly bag. Discard the rose petals. Measure the volume of liquid.

4. Add and equal amount of sugar to the liquid in the saucepan. Heat over medium heat until sugar is dissolved.

5. Bring syrup to a boil.

6. Remove pan from heat. Cool. Store in a capped bottle in the refrigerator.

7. The syrup will keep in the refrigerator for a month or so. For longer storage, pour syrup into ice cube trays and freeze. Keep in a zip top bag and thaw as needed.

Makes about 3 cups of syrup.

Boiled Apple-Pear Syrup

Fortunately, I live in an area that grows lots and lots of apple varieties. I don't have any apple trees myself, but always have a plethora of options at the Farmer's Market. And if I am willing to purchase apples with scars and a few bruises I can get them for around fifty cents per pound.

It's hard to turn down this great offer so I often go home with 25 pounds of apples. Then reality sets in, "I have to process all these apples!"

Over the years I have dried apples, made applesauce, cooked with apples – a lot – and even canned the occasional jar of apple-plum jelly. But one year I made Boiled Apple-Pear Syrup.

Boiled Apple-Pear Syrup is similar to boiled apple cider. No sugar is added to Boiled Apple-Pear Syrup. All of the sweetness comes from the fruits' natural sugars.

Boiled Apple-Pear Syrup can be used anywhere you would use molasses, honey, or boiled apple cider:

- Glaze for donuts or baked ham
- Added to homemade applesauce or apple pie
- Substituted for molasses in fruitcake
- Added to sugar cookies
- Served over pancakes or pork chops
- Added to homemade vinaigrette
- Drizzled over Apple-Pear Crisp

- 4 LBS APPLES, ANY VARIETY OR A COMBINATION
- 4 LBS PEARS, ANY VARIETY OR A COMBINATION

1. Wash but do not peel or core the fruit. Cut into quarters. Place all the fruit in a large slow-cooker. Cook on low overnight or at least 10 hours.

2. Drain and press the fruit. I did this in batches using a cheesecloth lined colander over a large bowl to catch the juice.

3. Pour the juice into a medium sized saucepan. Boil gently, stirring occasionally until syrup is dark and thick, 20 – 40 minutes.

4. Pour syrup into a clean jar. Cover and store in the refrigerator. Syrup should keep for up to 3 months, if you can refrain from using it all before then!

Makes about 1 pint.

Apricot Cognac Ginger Conserve

Conserves are similar to jams and preserves. They were very popular in Victorian England, but are almost forgotten today.

Technically conserves should contain nuts, raisins or other dried fruit along with fresh fruit suspended in a thickened syrup. But not all recipes call for these ingredients, and really – who is going to argue about the technical points of sweet spreads?

This particular recipe was developed one of those years when the apricots were plentiful. It would be equally good made with peaches.

Serve spread on a ham and Swiss sandwich for a gourmet treat.

INGREDIENTS

- 2 LBS APRICOTS, CHOPPED
- 3 CUPS GRANULATED SUGAR
- ¼ CUP COGNAC
- 2 TBSP CHOPPED CANDIED GINGER

1. Add the apricots and sugar to a large saucepan.
2. Slowly bring the mixture to a boil over medium heat, stirring until sugar is dissolved.
3. Add Cognac and ginger.

4. Turn the heat up a little and cook rapidly, stirring often to prevent sticking, until it reaches the gelling point.

5. Use the plate method to check for gelling or use a digital thermometer. Gelling is reached at 220 degrees or 8 degrees above the boiling point of water.

6. Spoon the hot jam into prepared jars, leaving ¼ inch head space.

7. Wipe the lip of each jar with a damp paper towel, top the jars with a lid and a lid ring.

8. Process the jars in a water bath canner for 10 minutes. Remove and let cool completely.

Makes about 5 half-pints.

Meyer Lemon Marmalade with Honey

Marmalade seems to be one of those things you either love or hate. I am firmly in the first category. But I don't make marmalade very often because there aren't many marmalade fans in the family.

This recipe might just change their minds. Unlike traditional Seville Orange marmalade which is quite bitter, Meyer Lemon marmalade is just the right combination of sweet and tart and bitter.

What are Meyer Lemons?

Meyer lemons are supposedly a cross between an everyday lemon and a Mandarin orange (better known as a tangerine). Their skin is thinner than a regular lemon and has an orange blush.

Meyer lemons are sweeter than lemons but not as sweet as tangerines. They can usually be found in the produce section, often bagged in one-pound bags.

Making Marmalade with Honey

I love using honey in my sweet spreads. Honey adds a mellowness that can't be found when using sugar alone. Be sure to use a mild flavored honey here as we still want the lemon flavor to shine through. Orange blossom honey would be perfect, but wildflower or clover honey is nice also. The important thing is to use a good quality honey.

INGREDIENTS

- 1 LB MEYER LEMONS
- 2 ⅔ CUPS WATER
- 1 ⅓ CUP GRANULATED SUGAR
- 1 ⅓ CUP HONEY

1. Wash lemons. Trim ends.

2. Cut lemons into wedges and then thinly slice wedges crosswise.

3. Combine lemon slices and water. Let sit 8 hours or overnight.

4. Add sugar and honey to lemon mixture.

5. Slowly bring mixture to a boil, stirring occasionally.

6. Cook rapidly until mixture reaches the gelling point, about 220 degrees. This will take approx. 25 minutes.

7. Spoon marmalade into clean, ½ pint jars. Top with two-piece caps.

8. Process in a water bath canner for 10 minutes.

Makes 4 half-pints.

Kumquat Vanilla Marmalade

Here in the Mid-Columbia we suffered through the worst winter in decades. It started snowing in early December and didn't stop for months. Let me rephrase that – it didn't stop until it started showering down freezing rain instead! Then another half-inch of fluffy, white snow - on a day when the forecast called for 0% chance of precipitation. I guess weather forecasting isn't an exact science.

Now this shouldn't be an issue, except that I really dislike winter. Luckily, I work from home and don't have to venture out onto the slushy, icy roads. But then I feel trapped. The best way to ameliorate this feeling is to cook. So, when I saw Marisa McClellan of **Food in Jars** fame launch a new Mastery Challenge, I jumped. I was especially thrilled that January's challenge was Marmalade.

What Are Kumquats?

Kumquats are cute little citrus fruits. They look like miniature oranges, ones you would perhaps find in a fairy garden. Like most citrus, they arrive in the grocery stores around the holidays. Kumquats are meant to be eaten whole, peel and all. Although they are sweeter than eating a whole orange, the peel still has a bitter-sour edge to it. Kumquats go well with other seasonal fruit like cranberries, papaya and oranges.

Making the Marmalade

Marmalade requires a bit more attention than jam-making, but you don't have to be an expert cook to make your own batch. Plus, it's the perfect project if you are getting itchy to start canning season. The finished jars are a transparent golden yellow jelly, dotted with the black vanilla, surrounding the miniature kumquat "wheels."

INGREDIENTS

- 1 LB FRESH KUMQUATS, WASHED AND SLICED IN ROUNDS
- 3 CUPS WATER
- 3 CUPS GRANULATED SUGAR
- 1 VANILLA BEAN

1. Combine sliced kumquats and water in a large saucepan or Dutch oven.
2. Let sit 8 hours or overnight.
3. Add sugar and slowly bring mixture to a boil, stirring occasionally.
4. Scrape the vanilla bean and add the paste to the marmalade.
5. Cook rapidly until it reaches the gelling point, about 220 degrees.
6. Spoon marmalade into clean, ½ pint jars. Top with two-piece caps.
7. Process in a water bath canner for 10 minutes.

Makes 3 half-pints.

CHAPTER SEVEN
Resources

Resources Mentioned in This Book

Websites:

SeedtoPantry.com: Renee Pottle

FoodinJars.com: Marisa McClellan

PunkDomestics.com: Sean Timberlake

Books:

The Confident Canner: Answers to Your Canning Questions; by Renee Pottle

The Ball Blue Book

The Joy of Jams, Jellies, and Other Sweet Preserves; by Linda Ziedrich

Recipes:

Cherries Chicken Jubilee recipe and

Apple-Pear Crisp recipe can be found at
www.SeedtoPantry.com

Canning Gifts:

Visit our **Etsy shop** for canning related gifts, including a downloadable **Canning Journal.**

www.etsy.com/shop/SeedtoPantry

More Canning Tips:

Sign up for our monthly newsletter and receive monthly tips and recipes. www.SeedtoPantry.com

Customer Bonuses

Thank you for purchasing this book.

If you enjoyed it, please consider writing an **Amazon.com** or other review. We small, home-based writers and publishers greatly appreciate your help spreading the word about our books. Don't worry if you aren't an experienced writer; simply saying, "I liked it and this is why" will help your fellow readers.

Bonuses:

More Sweet Treats Recipes

Additional Jammy Creations Recipes

20% off of a future order

Get your bonuses here!

www.seedtopantry.com/creative-jams-and-preserves-bonus-page/

About the Author

A frugal Yankee at heart, Renee first learned to can as a child; hanging out in her Nana's kitchen while she and her sisters gossiped and put up jars and jars of pickles.

Later, Renee would sneak into the basement to view numerous colorful jars of carrots, green beans, tomatoes and other garden bounty. It was a lesson learned quite young – growing and preserving it yourself saves money, and tastes like Nana's love!

Before she knew it, Renee was a wife and mother with a kitchen of her own. A slim wallet and a child who couldn't tolerate food additives set her firmly on the food self-reliance path more than 30 years ago.

Since then she's been planting, foraging, and preserving, and turning her little ¼ acre house lot into a family food Eden.

Renee's passion for food preservation, and the science behind it, eventually led her to an exciting and multifaceted career as:

- Published Author of several cookbooks
- Home Economist/Family and Consumer Scientist
- Master Food Preserver/Food Safety Advisor
- Nutrition Heath Educator
- Freelance Food Writer and Recipe Developer

Renee and her husband make their home in Kennewick, Washington where their two sons, daughters-in-law and grandchildren visit often to raid the jelly cupboard.

www.ingramcontent.com/pod-product-compliance
Lightning Source LLC
Chambersburg PA
CBHW021200020426
42331CB00003B/140